In *Altar for Broken Things*, Deborah Miranda acknowledges and witnesses this broken world and the wounds we all carry, and shows both the struggles and the transformations into beauty and compassion. Miranda finds the sacred everywhere: in an acorn—"the sound inside you is sacred", and in the persistence of the living world—"Oysters still meld/smooth jewels/from sharp intrusions/filter and cleanse/the world's weary waters." These poems are pearls built around the wounds we all carry, personally and culturally; this voice is one that cleanses. Miranda's poems are prayers sung in harmony with the other-than-human world, and with all those who protect and resist, poems that proclaim that the "earth itself is a prayer." Miranda writes in the tradition of ecstatic poets, celebrating the sacred, which is not separate from ourselves, but is the matrix within which we live. Still, Miranda reminds us, despite everything, the world is "sweet, sweet, sweet." The erotic, that deep current of life and spirit that runs through the living world—and everything is included in that living world—flows through these poems, subverts the destruction of colonialism and greed, and insists on sovereignty—of the earth, of Native nations, of all persons. This volume is a generous gift to all of us who are struggling in this time to find our way to healing, back to the sacred, back to hope.

—Cheryl Savageau, *Out of the Crazywoods*

Altar for Broken Things

Also by Deborah A. Miranda

Bad Indians: A Tribal Memoir
Raised by Humans
Indian Cartography
Zen of La Llorona

Altar for Broken Things

poems

Deborah A. Miranda

BkMk Press
University of Missouri-Kansas City
www.bkmkpress.org

BkMk Press
University of Missouri-Kansas City
5101 Rockhill Road
Kansas City, Missouri 64110
www.bkmkpress.org

Executive Editor: Christie Hodgen
Mananging Editor: Ben Furnish
Assistant Managing Editor: Cynthia Beard

Author photo: Margo Solod

Partial support for this project has been provided by the Missouri Arts
Council, a state agency.

See page 109 for a complete list of donors to BkMk Press.

Library of Congress Cataloging-in-Publication Data

Names: Miranda, Deborah A., author.
Title: Altar for broken things : poems / Deborah Miranda.
Description: Kansas City, Missouri : BkMk Press, University of
  Missouri-Kansas City, [2020] | Summary: "These poems explore
  interlocking themes of sacrifice-willing and forced-and the sacred
  dimension of nature and the need for spiritual healing in a world
  suffering from the aftereffects of slavery and genocide, as well as
  homophobia and environmental damage. Many of the poems describe subjects
  in the Virginia Appalachian region as well as the author's indigenous
  Ohlone-Costanoan Esselen California coastal homeland"-- Provided by
  publisher.
Identifiers: LCCN 2020044389 | ISBN 9781943491261 (paperback)
Subjects: LCGFT: Poetry.
Classification: LCC PS3563.I688 A79 2020 | DDC 811/.54--dc23
LC record available at https://lccn.loc.gov/2020044389

ISBN 978-1-943491-26-1

Dedication

For our elders Isabel, Ursula, and Ruth.
You have gone on, but your work remains,
still teaching us how to make beauty from the broken pieces.
Gratitude.

For three new grandsons Jhonathan, Danny, and James.
Our mosaic artists.
Love.

Contents

THE HAND OF GOD

PRAYER OF PRAYERS

altar

n.

Old English *alter*, *altar*, from Latin *altare* (plural *altaria*) "high altar, altar for sacrifice to the great gods," perhaps originally meaning "burnt offerings" (cf. Latin *adolere* "to worship, to offer sacrifice, to honor by burning sacrifices to").

How to Love the Burning World

... is it still possible to face the gathering darkness, and say to the physical Earth, and to all its creatures, including ourselves, fiercely and without embarrassment, I love you, and to embrace fearlessly the burning world?
—Barry Lopez

Tell yourself it's like sitting at the bedside
of your mother; scorched with cancer,
her hand already almost ash in yours,
her words already smoke so thick
it obscures your vision of a future
without her. You want to look away.
You want to find a cave, drink yourself
into oblivion, sleep while ugliness smolders.
Admit it. You want someone else to tend
the deathwatch. Instead, moisten her tongue
with a sponge; bathe dry skin
with lavender cream; braid her hair
with tender, trembling fingers. Take care
not to pull on knots. Stay in the room:
let the last thing she hears
be your voice, thanking her
for every single time she didn't
kill you, for the eons she waited
before you realized her brilliance,
her wisdom, all the days she bit
her tongue, let you think you had
the last bloody word.

You aren't required to love the flames.

But love the burning world.
You owe her that. Fear is no dishonor.
Her fever so hot even metaphors
melt at a touch. Memorize her.
Praise each scar on her body,

beauty ablaze. Pray for a clean
ending, a phoenix purification.
Pray for mercy. Pray for the only thing
that can save us now:
every lesson she ever taught us
about the sweet, bitter grace
of transformation.

BIRD CHURCH

Offerings

At dawn the songs begin again as if never sung before,
as if the jet stream has not wandered from its path,

the Arctic ice shelf does not melt at accelerated rates,
Sudden Oak Death does not leapfrog across the continent.

Shenandoah Valley songbirds lean into the indigo air
as if two thousand snow geese did not fall from the sky

in Idaho, ten thousand sea lions are not washing up dead
in the Channel Islands, train tanker cars full of chemicals

never crashed into the Kanawah River in West Virginia.
As if California's Central Valley agriculture is not pumping

twenty-thousand-year-old water out of ancient aquifers
that cannot be refilled. These song warriors pitch morning

as if the territorial prayers of robins keep bee-colony collapse
disorder at bay, as if crows stitch each torn morning together

with their black beaks, mockingbirds know the secret
combination of notes that command God's ear, the low *coo*

of mourning doves weaves feathery medicine; they persist
as if pine warblers, flash of gold in treetops, coax the sun

up by degrees, as if these musical beings don't know the word
extinction, as if, knowing it, their silvered melodies insist

like the yellow warbler: *sweet-sweet-sweet; little-more-sweet.*

Acorn

That sound inside you is sacred:
heartbeat of a seed eager to emerge.

That sound inside you is urgent:
life's sharp, percussive pulse.

That sound inside you is the future,
rattling a polished brown shell

shaped like a goddess, or breast.
You are what Jesus meant when he said

the meek shall inherit the Earth. You
are what Hillel had in mind when he said,

this is the whole Torah. Ah, secret
begging to be told, treasure whispering

find me. You are the Creator's fingerprint
left behind in soft red clay, hardening in sun,

the sleek amulet snug in my palm,
ripe mother of nations.

From your flesh comes all words
for holiness, celebration, awe.

Palatsa, little rattle, you hold time in your belly—
round and full and kicking its way into life.

Taksita

No one speaks
    my real name
        anymore. Maybe it's gone
           on to the next world
                where no spirit
                    fears dam
                          or drought
                  —I'm still here—
                a little
          lonesome
              for
        that
        language
        I do
    my work
    succor
      snapping
    turtles
          in soft mud
              tickle fat
                  catfish
                  whiskering
              along mossy stones
                    heron's
            long legs
            weave
                through my reeds,
                delicate dance
                  of the hunt
                  my currents carve
                      deep cold kettles
                  where trout circle
                  like secret

                                        jewels
                            stone spirits
                        crouch
                    in the darkest
                    pools,
                            silent beauties
                                in the shape of fate
                        if this is not grace
                tell me what is
        if I am not a god
            tell me who is?
                            Some-
                            times
                    when I am
                            a little too full
                        of myself
                    the mountains
                        remind me:
                                I still rock
                                in the cradle
                        of my mother
                    I belong
            to her—
        not the other
    way
    around.

Tears of the Sun

In 1785, a Chumash woman at Mission Santa Barbara had a vision: the earth goddess Chupa told her that Indians who chose to remain Catholic, as baptized by the mission priests, would die—but those who bathed in the "'tears of the sun'" could escape the bonds of that baptism and return to their former state as free souls.

The river swirls with mica.
We submerge our bodies;

she wraps us in constellations
of stars. Our forearms swirl

and sparkle like the Milky Way,
legs glint with galaxies.

Our hands glitter gold as if dipped
in stardust. October's sun scatters

sparks of the cosmos,
bathes us in the dust of all

that has come before. See
us: live embers cradling

the kindling that ignites.
See how the river dresses us—

lost, stolen, dispossessed, broken—
in quickening bones of granite,

souls of our Ancestors rising.

Eastern Box Turtle
(Terrapene peregrinus temporalis)

They meet on the mountain, carrying orange, yellow
and black calligraphy through October rain.

Male and female, elastic necks stretch out in prehistoric
passion beneath silvery leaves: concave lower plate

presses against carapace. Puzzle pieces, twin halves,
they've roamed the underbrush looking for this *yes*.

Her tail sweeps to one side, his rear plastron lowers,
back legs link. Lust holds them steady; claws rake top shell,

carve wet red clay. Topaz eyes dazzle like tiny suns.
Their hunger persists on convoluted ridges of oak and pine,

cedar and alder; endures separate solitudes under thick
wineberry and blackberry vines; navigates granite slabs,

a creek wandering through whole galaxies. Beaks bite,
shells crack—this is no tame lovemaking—the male rises

on the stiff back edge of his shell, thrusts in slow motion.
It's late in the season, but female turtle, old soul, survivor,

makes of herself a living time portal; stores her mate's seed
in her body's secret compartment. All winter, she'll hibernate

inside a hollowed-out space in the heart of the forest. By spring,
her mate may be far away, mounting some other fiery sister.

It won't matter. When she is ready, this small mountain
of a mother will unfreeze time, let egg and sperm rendezvous.

In the saddle between Big House and Little House Mountains
she'll dig her nest on a humid summer night. In due time, small

slow pilgrims will plow their way out from the earth—
each hatchling choosing a direction, each soul setting off to scale

what can't be scaled. Each shell bearing black brushstrokes:
a scripture of blessings for traveling through time.

My Crow

I know I'll travel to heaven in the guts of a crow—
each of us assigned transportation at birth, marked

upon our arrival in smoggy cities, cold mountains, lakes,
parking lots. That's why God made so many crows, you see:

no body forgotten, no flesh left undigested. A time to live,
a time to die, a time to re-enter Creation through

the lift of blackest feathers. I can pick my crow out
of a crowd despite identical sleek pinions

and black beaks clacking—he's something special, not
like the other trash-picking, dirt-talking, rabble-rousing

wannabes, ganging up on juveniles too big for the nest,
too thin for the flock. My crow stands alone on the bright yellow

centerline, guards fresh possum guts, raccoon entrails
sticky as glue, splattered deer brains; he doesn't flinch

as I draw closer in my big steel and plastic boat on wheels.
I can't stare him down; he's just doing his job: recycling

what's too slow, too old, too stupid to live, and I,
I am simply the one he's got his eye on next.

Not today, but thank you, I say as we pass: *Keep up
the good work without me, brother.*

Intention

A tulip poplar blossom
falls into my open palm:
cool cup, creamy
center with a ragged
ring of flame.

It has lived in the canopy
where the bees came
in their golden bodies,
filled their saddlebags
with pollen, carried it home
to the hive. All winter,
they'll consume this memory
—the sable, smoky taste
of a tree transformed
into light.

I want to go like that: a flowery
comet shooting slowly
across the dawn sky,
drenched in hungry kisses;
drifting into an open hand,
placed gently on the earth—
one small offering

upon the altar.

Scar

Autumn olives suture
I-81's shoulder, silver
and jade leaves wielding
stiletto thorns.

Wild garlic in patches
big as ponds glisten
like mossy mirages.

A red fox tucks himself
into a cedar hollow,
watches me flash past.

Bullets of yearning,
Red-tailed hawks scout
from the tops of pines,
feathers groomed
to a sharp crease.

Like a swarm of honeybees,
yellow sweet clover
rides the emerald swells
of fields behind barbed wire.

Blackberry vines surge
against a downed tree,
long dark suckers seeking
any anchor.

Seventy-seven different
shades of spring;
a million hosannas
from cuts of blue and gray stone
as I travel the length
of this old wound

one more time.

Gloaming

She looks up from the pages of a book:
the evening light has turned green.
Emanating from grass, tall spiky reeds,
fronds of black walnut trees brushing
the pond's surface; from water hyacinths,
teal needles of spruce, pine; from heavy
cedar boughs, mossy banks. The world,
mirrored in water, shines into shimmering,
verdant air. For a moment, she thinks a mist
has risen out of the earth, or drifted
down from confused, sea-foam clouds—
but it is only a thousand shades of life
bursting, bleeding, breathing. Listen:
this is photosynthesis but it is also magic.
This is science but it is sacred; mundane,
but also miracle. Fish with emerald
scales leap after jade dragonflies.
Heron preens in her iridescent sage
cloak. A khaki bullfrog croaks once,
deep in his throat: the sound green makes
when green speaks its name.

What Whales Want

What if we could swim oceans?
What if *home* meant water, darkness,
depth? What if air were precious scarce
and our hearts beat sleepy slow

in time with each blessed breach?
What if we circled continents
like currents, our bodies indifferent
to land, property, gold; what if

what mattered were only the taste
of one sea or the next, pull of moon,
a song made up between birthing
and weaning babes? What if

that were our world—
and all we needed,
all we wanted to know,
was how to do it well?

La Arribada

—*for Suzanne*
Sea turtles come ashore en masse, known as la arribada—*the arrival.*

She's a creature of cool blues,
warm greens, darkness; she's dazed
by sunlight. Angel of grace, barely touched
by gravity's cruel chains, she gives up
heaven for this moment: blind devotion
to heated sand, the weight of centuries.
Egg after egg falls into a nest
she will not visit again. This is faith.
Carrying her children this far,
no farther. They must want life enough
to find it on their own: earn the deepness
where they'll grow wings, where flight
is the native language. For now, she spreads
a smooth blanket over their coiled beginnings,
turns away, plows her path home. Time
drinks in her body like stars.

Looking for a River

We pass the long blue and white
tent, chairs set in sedate rows,
men and women silent shadows

in the heat; preparing for a revival,
they pay us no mind as our car
tires whine past on soft asphalt.

A bay horse grazes in a field. Black
Angus stand belly-deep in a farm pond,
tails switching flies, heads heavy,

somnolent statues cut out of starless
skies. On and on we drive, a little lost,
following the tendrils of a shaky map.

We're looking for a river. We're looking
for an incredulous current, sand soft as a kiss,
a hover of trout circling the kettle.

We're looking for the long white banner
of a waterfall, the hidden path behind
a plume of mist and ragged lace.

When we get there, we'll slide across
slick gray rocks, push aside moss
cascading out of deep cracks like prophets.

We'll crawl into that cool dark space
behind the veil, listen to the river preach:
granite gospel from the mouth of a mountain.

Venice Beach

Turtle Woman wants bare feet on sand that goes on for miles,
hair whipped into knots by wind. She wants salt, bits of ancient

mountains between her teeth, old hand-painted VW vans
in parking lots, curtains made from thin beach towels.

She wants tattoos of dolphins and mermaids; Muscle Beach
strut and sweat, battle cries of seagulls, low fog blurring

waves. Turtle Woman wants to walk past decades of loss,
past erasure. She wants to walk so far, so long that she walks

right around the spiral of history, back into that black and white
snapshot taken in 1962: her first wobbly steps on this beach,

where blue water baptized her into a tribe, named her
with a blood-sister vow. Turtle Woman wants the smell

of exile scratched off her skin, wants to smell like ocean,
like history. Like home.

Bird Church

Here I am, Lord.
I've come to worship
where you weave hymns
out of dried grass,
string, and dog hair,
where sacred texts trill
and whistle, where wings
carve praise out of wind.

Here I am, Lord, mourning
the death of three newly
hatched robins in yesterday's
hellish heat—
celebrating the miraculous
deliverance of a fourth.

Here I am in this cusp,
this dewy rapture we call *dawn*,
where every heart is green
and composed in hope's hand;
here I am, before the news cycle's
first blow, before I lose my way,
before I forget to duck.

Here I am at that threshold
when the world can still be saved.
Here I am, Lord, in the borderlands
of the day: Here, I am.

ALTAR FOR BROKEN THINGS

Corazón Espinado

In the beginning
she is salt, indigo and jade,
fire and magma.

She is prowl and push.
Land births herself:
eruptions red as first blood

accordion into ridges,
braids and breakage,
until wind and water

cool her ropey coils,
black body baptized,
lifted above the horizon.

Here, God is a seed
sown by chance.
Here, rock is womb.

Fine silvery roots spin
a seedling: world-maker,
queen born of water,

she grows her own
green heart of spines
crowned with golden jewels.

Questions About Lightning

She knows it's about collision,
temperature, water. Tiny droplets,
ice crystals, small pellets
of hail, a hot streak of plasma—
that extraterrestrial, whirling
ionized gas found
in faraway stars. But what
force makes the hairs
along the back of her neck
rise as if in worship?
Whose face does she recognize
inside stacked clouds
above her, now bruised green,
now lavender, now dizzy yellow?
Do strikes blaze
a kind of cosmic code
across the prairie,
scrawl like gospel or graffiti?
What symbols sizzle
on her tongue?

She knows a twin storm
circulates in her heart's
sinoatrial node; strands
of magic burst and dart
from one cell to the next,
command blood, breath,
thought—messengers
quick as angels
with electric-blue wings.
What if prairies flash
like that, a pulse firing
from the heart of an entity

the size of a planet? What if
this land and her body
bear the same jagged scripture?
Would she disappear into
a story too large for human
souls to comprehend? Or
would she, finally, see?

Still

1.

Somedays I think
about the feral hunger
loose in this world:
fear of emptiness,
fear of never filling up,
Horror vacui.

Some nights
I remember those men
whose hunger
stalked me,
told me I was smart,
pretty, the one,
the only one.

When I remember how
they devoured me,
chewed me up,
swallowed me
to ease
their own bottomless
need,

I want to never
be beautiful
again.

2.

Bees still pollinate
the poisoned world,
rear translucent generations
in exquisite,
hexagonal wombs.

Oysters still meld
smooth jewels
from sharp intrusions,
filter and cleanse
the world's weary waters.

3.

I don't have a word
for fear of my own beauty.
But this much is true:
a monstrous hunger
sometimes steals what glory
we possess,
leaves our bodies
lost, torn.
I've traced
those tooth marks
on my skin.

I want a map
back from the belly
of someone else's
emptiness.

4.

Pearls and honey,
honey and pearls.

If I chose faith,
if I gave
my allegiance
to awe's
iridescent scar,
would that redeem
the blood of flowers?

Companion

Talk to me
about loneliness.

I've seen the way you run
your hand across her soft gray pelt

absentmindedly, as rain comes down
outside the walls of your house

way out on the edge
of the known world. I've

heard you singing to her
late at night, your family

asleep in other rooms,
their beloved bodies curled

under quilts and cedar-scented
dreams. You know more about her

than you let on. I've seen that scar
on the back of your neck

where loneliness picked you up
like a stray cub, shook you hard,

knocked you back on your heels.
Her teeth marked you, didn't they?

Loneliness got into your blood.
Now she walks around inside you.

Tell me how to live
with a ghost who's never there;

not the shadow you were born with,
but the one that found you.

Step into the Blur

—for Ursula, ukuski-koltala tanoch

Stand firm
in your body
if darkness falls.
Cocoon
your soul, swaddle it, strap it
to your chest.
Your heart
learns faith like a song,
each note a revelation.
Realize: you stand
at the edge of all maps.
Fear is your scout.
You carry
your own light like a flint.
Strike that stone
within you;
sparks fly out, seek tinder,
catch fire.
In the blur
you do not fear dragons.
Trust your wings.

Out on the edge,
you *are*
the dragon.

Adiositos

The sky lightens
in the east,
incandescent promise
under a thin cloud cover.
I think of our walks,
those dawns, those risings.

The earth turns
toward Spring,
thunder rumbles
all day. Thank you
for your dear words.
Write to me about rivers.

Remember, everything
was green, wet, dripping—
we found a lush stand
of huckleberries down
by the creek. How they
glowed: red, fat, like
salmon eggs. We filled
our hands easily,
greedy little bears.

On my walk at lunch, I saw
two great blue herons
flying low over a blue
pond. A red fox sauntering
along a deer trail,
muzzle testing the air;
a loud swarm of bees
clustered in a pine.

You said it was like eating rain.

Three hours before sunset
now—a sweet time. Such
colors in the earth: deep
browns, ochres, yellows,
pale gray, hearty greens.
Broken clouds;
farther north, a hard
fist of cloud,
full of lightning.

Evening in the hills.
Darkness coming on quick
as crickets. Clouds
the color of jacaranda
blossoms. A little windy,
but soft. Smoke
from someone's
fireplace whispers
in my mouth.
Mourning doves
in the cedars
coo and whistle—
old songs
from my childhood.

Big streaks of light
under cumulus clouds;
I could almost walk up
those fat beams, roads
into the sky. When you
read this,
remember—

Very full and strange
over those open meadows
to the east—la luna—

—*things don't die,*
amorcita. We
won't die.

　　　　—she's far away
　　　　from her mother,
　　　　from home—

We'll transform.

That Word

—with thanks to Mary TallMountain

It rings through the cave of my body
like a bell with a solid stone clapper,

ceaseless echo—each abandonment a shot
that ricochets off ribs, pelvis,

vertebrae, skull until I am nothing
but a pinball machine of departures,

heart smacked and jarred by electricity,
teeth buzzing with all not spoken—

no, there is no word for *good-bye*:
just one heart always tucked

inside another. Micha ene hikpalala:
I'll see you soon.

Elegy for a Nomad

You must call out
her name
six times.

Whisper it
the way you did
that first time
you saw her
under dark pines
on a June evening,
your mouth full
of wild lilies
and pollen.

Howl her name
like a river hellbent
for the rapids,
like a curse;
the way you said it
the moment she placed
herself on the altar
of your heart.

Shape her name
like a shroud
woven of silk;
wrap each syllable
in the caress
left behind, hidden
in the crevices
of your body.

Sing her name,
the secret one;
swallow the echo

you fell into the day
she left for good
and you keened
like a child,
like a storm.

Bite her name;
chew its red letters
like the gifts
you burned or buried—
Chimayo weaving,
Hopi corn plant
etched in silver,
sweet ashes
lingering like grit
in your teeth.

Cradle her name
on your tongue
for the last time,
sharp edges burning.
Open your mouth—
her name leaps
from your lips,
a star shooting
in the direction
her light always
yearned to go,
the spiraled road
that leads away.

Questions About the Afterlife

Where do you walk now?
What new maps have you drawn,

or have you left maps behind?
How is your heart? Does turquoise

in a stone or lake still bring you joy?
Wars have ended, and begun,

since your soul and body parted ways.
Trees have fallen in brutal derechos,

acorns burrowed into the soft earth
with one green root. I have slept,

and dreamt, and walked in rain;
my skin has burnt, healed,

darkened. A million words
swarm around me, but

I do not know if any of mine
reach you, nor do I have any of yours

to hold to my heart and praise.
Are you humming as you travel?

Which road will you take next?
Do you think of me?

I keep your memory
like a singing cricket

on the hearth of my heart.
All I know for sure:

those notes, steady as footsteps,
will outlive both of us.

Hagiography

—with thanks to Kimiko Hahn

In the cathedral of childhood, your mother's altar
glitters at the center of a dark dais. You worship
that cold figure—suffering writ upon her adored
body. Fine lines like dry streams across her pale
forehead, sunken cheeks, red lips pursed around
an eternal cigarette, crutch she cannot cast away.
Silent as an unrung bell, she is her own shadow.

In this cathedral, flakes of stained glass bleed
the many scenes of your mother's torments—
red, indigo, gold, green, blue welded together
with thick lines of lead; ritual scarification.
You know each story, kneel in horror before
her miraculous birth, the caustic sacrifices,
holocaust of cancer. In between, a life spent

burning. Here in this cathedral, eternal neophyte,
you recite the creed: if she does not love you,
you're to blame; if she does love you, it is not
that you are worthy—merely the miracle
of her martyred, absent-minded grace.

The Blow

—for my father

Hurricanes that wallop out of season;
wasps in among blackberries, dead silent
until touched. Loaning out your own best skin
for one night to a dear friend, finding your beauty
torn and tattered in the trash. A promise
metastasizes into haunted moan,
hope gone sour as milk. Now we're getting close.
Homemade bread harboring a fateful stone,
end of the world coming at dawn, in May;
robins waking wet fields, honeysuckle
splayed starry, sinless as Eden's first day—
and then, the venom, poison that cuckolds:
the hero stepping out of soft gray mist,
a kiss in the shape of a fist.

All One

Origin and etymology of ALONE:
Middle English, from all + one

Turtle Woman comes
to you the way storms
are drawn to mountain tops,
wondering if her own
lightning strikes
will destroy her.

Sometimes love
is a leather belt,
singing. Sometimes,
love speaks from inside
a brown beer bottle.
Sometimes love waits
for a ride home
that never comes.

Turtle Woman thinks
her body is poisoned,
or poison. For years
she brings you her scars:
arms and legs, belly
with its stretch marks,
knotted feet,
shameful breasts,
jumbled parts—
at the bottom
of the pile, she hides
her wide hips,
her sex shadowed
in between like a curse.

Finally, all she has left
are eyes that cry and cry,

a mouth that talks
and talks.
Those will be
the next to go.

Turtle Woman
is looking
for a savior
and it's not you;
saviors don't work
this hard. Follow her
right up to the edge
of the Pit, the place she lived
as a child; watch as she leaves
behind sleep, amnesia,
silence, absence,
any chemical
that might let her
escape.

Stand guard
as Turtle Woman lowers
herself down,
slides over
the slick edge.
She carries the thin
silken rope
the two of you
wove together,
hours of braiding
and unbraiding until
it bears her weight
without a tear.

Turtle Woman
dismembered herself
in order to survive
but now she pulls her limbs
from the Pit,
tries on an arm, a hand,
like somebody else's clothing.
You help her lift,
move, shift, imagine.
Re-membering herself
is a fearful task

but she's beginning to see

All one is a painful work of art;
alone does not mean
abandoned.

Altar for Broken Things

Sea snail shells bleached white by salt
and sun, jagged neck of a dusty pot, bottles
pounded, ground into pale green pebbles;
she collects survivors. Tattered feathers,
splinters of wood, the tokens of old lovers
thrown against the wall. She honors them all,
veterans of chance. Damaged things she can't let go:
no replacement, no salvation. This is the altar
of the almost-lost, way station between found
and forgotten, or forgiven. She reveres ruins:
creatures caught in their worship of waves,
hollow-boned birds chasing hurricane winds.
Perfection is the gift best given away. Better
cracked open, storied by the world's
rough hands than left whole, wholly without
history. This altar testifies to the only thing
she ever decided to abandon: regret.

THE HAND OF GOD

God's House

Imagine the inside of a sand dollar:
arches rising to a peaked roof, light
streaming in through tiny holes.

Turtle Woman looks for that cathedral
everywhere. Tries Assembly of God,
St. Stephen's, Temple Beth El.

Lets Mormon sisters named Betty,
Linda, and Rita show her how to fold
her arms and pray. Reads her mother's

books: *Seth Speaks, Silva Mind Control,
Jonathan Livingston Seagull*. Reads King
James, The Torah, The Gnostics.

Turtle Woman never was any good
at reading maps but she knows God's house
isn't in the hot, black-topped trailer park

where an old man in a two-tone
blue and white Chevy offers little girls
25 cents in exchange for a kiss.

Not at Vacation Bible School
in between popsicle-stick-and-yarn
God's eyes and Jesus Loves Me.

Not under the turquoise sting
of the swimming pool's beguiling
waters that nearly claim her breath.

Maybe God is homeless. Turtle Woman
wonders, is that God's blue tarp
under the trees beside the Interstate?

She imagines God hauling a rusty cart
over curbs, fighting for the last bed
at a shelter down on First Ave. Maybe

God's in line with her uncles and brother
down at the YMCA, waiting for a turn
in the shower. Maybe God just packed up,

moved on to a cheaper neighborhood.
Turtle Woman sighs: she's tired of looking.
Maybe she'll build God a tiny house,

an invitation, an altar, down on the beach
where the tide does baptisms twice daily,
and the sky is a dome full of saints.

Careless Atlantic

I find you washed up on an island
whose Wampanoag name means
end of the earth, hold your cool
alabaster weight in one hand,
consult the cracked map of your skin.

Heart, you've seen some action.
Heart, you've been around
this world a time or two.
Your bright skin carries
the green scent of other oceans.
You're not amulet or trinket;
not the kind of heart
that lodges on land for long.

Let me trace your suave outline
a few minutes more;
as if I've been here waiting
since the last ice age, as if
you are the first heart
that ever kissed my palm.

How often will a woman
get to hold the heart of an ocean
in her hand, stand still
and let it
        break her?

Kakalu-ichi

Crow,
walking-on-earth-crow,
don't cry—
are you hungry, sister?

Shine your feathers
with that pretty beak:
be proud of your wings!
Come with me.

I've dreamt of you,
your black eyes,
your black tears.

Ichi,
let's go
make gossip in the sky.

Kakun, shekesipsha, shewker—
they will all cry with jealousy.

We will eat wind.
We will drink clouds.
We will not go back.
We will fly, dancing—

Let asumpalala sufuno
Let asumpalala koxno
Let asumpalala ashitapxu
Let asumpalala ashiyaxa

Ike, ichi!
Come sky dance with me.

Palimpsest

How does obsidian forget the hiss of magma?
How does water forget the cloud of its birth?

Can wild iris forget the dark belly of the bulb?
Does scar forget the torn, raw edge of flesh?

Hands that reached inside chaos, brought me out into the world.
Mouth that breathed into mine a language wild enough to wake me.

When does fire forget lightning? Should canyon forget river?
Might skin renounce fingerprint? Will honey deny the bee?

Don't ask me to forget. Don't tell me this is over.
Beneath sand and broken mountains,

even the Mojave remembers salt of a fickle sea.

Love in the Margins

Come on, shapeshifter—
I can't dance either.
But I want to hold

your shadowy body,
hum crooked tunes
into your abalone ear.

Out here on the edge,
desperadas don't always
make good lovers.

Sometimes our scars
match too well; touch
is barbed wire and border.

I'll try not to hide behind
my bruises if you'll
give me the hard gray line

of your shoulder.
Can't you hear
the cricket's ebbing

daysong? Let me
tuck that tidal melody
into the wine-colored

strands of your hair,
braid your name
with horizon's indigo

kiss. Glorious outlaws,
we've got nothing to lose
but this edge.

When You Forget Me

—with thanks to Pablo Neruda

The past is a poor broken basket,
woven by hands that had no muscle, no song.
When you forget me, every word we spoke together
just before or after slow first light, lips still wet,
—*doe, heron, stone, prayer*—erases itself
from every language, as if never spoken. Extinct.

When you forget me, dream of other women,
offer them the dance of your heart, recline
in a meadow, drink red wine, seek another woman's
blush, what basket could hold all this desire?
I'll gather black maidenhair fern stems, redbud,
bear grass from our sacred places; I'll harvest,
split and dry each piece. My busy hands
won't miss the obsidian outline of your face.

When you forget me, that river where we first kissed
won't stop flowing down from mountains older
than desire; when you forget me, the forest that cradled
our creation won't burn down. Some things last.
I'll remember what they are, one by one, as I dye
my bundles, start the coil, fit weft around stave.
I'll remember how to make a life out of fragments,
how to splice so skillfully, no visible break remains.

If I Say the Words

I read the reports, interviews with parents and children and lovers left behind. I read texts scrabbled out from hiding places, pleas for rescue, *call 911.*

My skin pricks and shivers as if someone touches me, but I am alone. I tear up at random times, can't bear to go out in public, see the world going on as if nothing happened, as if—because it didn't happen *here*—the bubble of denial still holds.

My wife and I pause, lean our bodies together. We say we are sad. Shorthand for *burned to the ground.*

I am full of the rough material that make up words—emotion, fear, grief—but the words themselves refuse to be born.

If I say the words, *say their names,* I admit that it happened.

Mercedez, Franky, Akyra, Eddie, Angel, all of them in their glorious brown queer radiant bodies—died in terror and agony, chased by a man wielding a SIG MCX Low-Visibility Assault Weapon. Nicknamed *Black Mamba,* never meant to hunt anything but human beings; it is a hate machine, created to shoot hatred from one person into the soft body of another.

If I say the words, if I try to corral facts and tame them with language, I've already muted their screams, their whispered prayers, their frantic messages to a beloved mami or daddy who cannot save their child.

If I say the words that attempt to respond to an act for which there is no sane response, what would those words be?

I think of Brenda: the mother out dancing with her son; *how lucky she was* to step in front of her child, face the shooter with her mother's eyes, shield her heart of hearts with the same body that gave birth to that boy.

That's it. That's what I see, over and over again, that is what I cannot speak, what terrifies me: how blessed she was, and is. She *already knew* that choosing love would save her son's life; knew that love, with its dance of blood and shattered bones, love with its twin red shoes named *pain* and *sacrifice*, is the only commandment that matters.

Love: by any means necessary.

January

Walking home late tonight
right in the center of the road,
I tip my head way back,
body open to blazing stars
as if someone
unzipped my skin
from head to toe,
exposed a naked captive
who'd only dreamt
of seeing sky.

For one clean moment
I am molten silver, pure
gratitude; I am light
calling to light, I am
light answering light.
For one moment
I have no name,
no past, no future,
no need. Then my street
rises up to greet me;
I stumble, find
the sidewalk,
hobble home—
stars seared into my retinas
like the after-image
of hope.

Bee Balm

—with thanks to Linda Hogan

On those days
when you return
home, soul dragging,
ashes of the world
in your teeth,
go unseal the jar;

dip your spoon
into that distilled
devotion; hold
that waxy sunlight
on your tongue.

Close your eyes:
tulip poplar, honeysuckle,
cedar, wild rose.

Let honey remind you
where you came from:
sweat and sweetness,
sweetness and sweat—

       all day long,
       the love of thousands.

Ursa Major

—for James

I stand beneath
a canopy of stars
on the edge
of the great plains
where the wind
blows like a giant
creature at full gallop

and from the southwest
comes coyote song,
a whole pack
of voices stitching
the blackness in crazed
silver threads.

I tilt my head back,
transfixed
beneath constellations
swimming from winter
into spring.

The old words to ease
a difficult birth
have not come down to me
so I invent them,
call it devotion
like every grandmother
who has ever walked
these plains.

I sing the Deer Song,
tender syllabics
meant to coax
and lure the shyest

creature out of hiding.
The coyotes
fall silent and the stars
might listen
as I sing and turn
in a full circle
on the eastern edge
of the great plains
while the U.S. flag
snaps in the wind
on its metal pole
at the Tippecanoe
County Library
across the street

in a country
where we shelter in place,
shelter in love –
oh grandchild,
won't you come out
tonight and dance
by the light
of this Bear?
I can't promise you much—
the memory
of tall grass,
tricksters at the margins,
night skies
full of ancestors

but I'll give you
the only power
I know, the only language

left to pass on—
none of this
metaphor; all of this,
all of it, mystery.

What the Shuttle Driver Told Me

My spiritual education began when I was broke, dead broke.
I lost my job. I had nothing. I went to a park,
sat down and cried.
A man in a black suit stopped in front of me.
    He said,
    I'm a magician.
    I have one trick no one else in the world can do.
    Watch.
    No, I won't explain. It's magic.
    God sent me to give you a blessing, he said:
    Don't worry about money.
    Oh, and feed the birds.

Three days in a row I sat on that bench.
Three days in a row, that magician found me.
Each time, he repeated his impossible trick.
I could never figure it out.
And he always had a big bag of bread
for the birds:
pigeons, crows, sparrows,
they waited for him.
Those birds knew him.

Growing up in El Salvador,
I used to catch little lizards and kill them.
I thought I was a hunter.
As an adult, I realize I've caused a lot of damage.
I have to pay it back.
That's one thing the magician taught me.
You know, you can feed a bunch of birds really fast, every day.
Little blessings—you can give them easily.
It's not that hard.
Every day I look for a new way.

Anyway, after the third visit from the magician,
I went back to the garage where I used to work;
I told the other mechanics about my magician.
One guy said:
    Oh! I know who you mean! He wears a top hat, right?
Yes, I said, and a long black overcoat too.
    Wait, when was this? My friend was looking at me funny.
Today, just now, I said, and for two days before that.
    Oh no, Eduardo, my friend laughed,
    That can't be right.
    That's old so-and-so (I can't remember his name), he was famous.
    He died ten years ago.

I've never seen that magician again.
Was he a ghost? a spirit? an angel?
I always remember what he said:
God sent me to give you a blessing.

I've never worried about money since then.
I've never been that penniless again.
He taught me how to give blessings.
I wish I had some rose quartz for you.
Rose quartz is for healing.
The first time I touched it, I fainted.
It was like an electrical shock.
Now I still tingle all over,
but my body absorbs the energy.
I'm hungry for it, like a vitamin.

—is this your destination?—
by the gate?
Sign here.
Take your receipt.
I'll remember you
in my prayers.
I would give you rose quartz
if I had any.

The Hand of God

Driving home,
the Blue Ridge mountains
stack up soft in this humid evening,
pierced by streaks of filtered light.
Someone's mother once called
these gold arrows
the hand of God. Of course,
the question is always,
whose God?

The backseat's filled
with bulk flours, walnuts,
sunflower and pumpkin seeds
from The Cheese Shop
where parking lot signs read

>"You shall not lie with a male
>as with a woman; it is an abomination"

>"The truth will set you free"

The question is still, whose truth?
Traveling silent now
beneath a luminous hand
that does not distinguish
between this body or that body,
this faith or that, this country
or another, I wonder: is there a God
worthy of old mountains, silvered clouds?
A God whose fingers stretch out,
caress us all? A God in the image
of the beloved? Whose God?

Nobody owns that mystery.

PRAYER OF PRAYERS

After Charlottesville

—with thanks to C. Rosalind Bell

Icebergs calve like this:
a glacier expands, groans,
a crevasse deepens, geometry
meets water pressure—
silent, unseen, ignored.

Thickness, impurity, stress
mix and protest, fist
thuds against its own body.

A crack like a sonic boom—
time hovers, holds its breath—
invisible knife cuts the cord.
Ice slams into water,
wave rises like a wall.

In all ways this is a birth,
a creature entering the fiery world
from an indigo-blue womb,
separation and creation
in one swift gasp.

Remember: beginnings emerge
out of endings. Today's blood
is tomorrow's inheritance.
We are the grownups now.

Almost Midnight

Wife and dogs sleep upstairs.
I sit here with the front door open.

Crickets sing patiently, a long lullaby
in lazy harmony. Rain falls

on our tin roof, sharp taps of reality,
start and stop. I breathe myself back

into my body. Come back, self. You've
been out fighting demons and bullies

and liars. You've been talking
to an electronic box with no ears.

You've been cheering for a democracy
that doesn't exist. We're all walking on bones.

Some of us are walking on more bones
than others. Breathe. Back into the body,

little one. The human world is broken,
but so beautifully. Corruption of the soul

never shows scars; when you don't resist,
no wounds exist. Breathe, breathe it back.

In this world, we live in bodies of flesh.
In this world our souls tether themselves

with blood. This is a good thing. Otherwise
we might take wing into darkness,

never touch our Mother, twist language
into silvery shapes. Breathe now. Let

the crickets tell you their truth.
Let it be yours, for now.

Things Fire Can't Destroy

Burn letters, books,
bridges. Burn down
a courthouse,
a church, a forest.
The human body
stores it all: the pistol of grief.
Fist of lust. Facts
of abandonment.
Wonder of scars.

Burn the body, then:
immerse it in fire. Use
the flamethrowers
of suicide: cocaine,
heroin, starvation.
Use tools of genocide:
smallpox, ovens.

In theory, if you burn
enough bodies, you can
incinerate memory.
Burn enough memories—
you can rewrite history.

In practice, memory lives on
in subterranean streams,
deep veins cut channels
into the next hidden spring.
Memory seeps like an oasis
waiting to wet the parched
throats of truthtellers
who go on, nesting one
inside the other,

like an egg inside
a lotus
inside
a phoenix.

26 Ways to Reinvent the Alphabet

Alphabet, you came for me
with a colonizer's awful generosity

You taught my small hand
how to carve the anchors
of my own missionized name

You loaned me your blocky shapes
so I could raise walls against monsters,
piece together little bridges
for my secrets to cross over

No one listened
like you, Alphabet

I strapped my burdens
to your back in baskets
composed of grief
and you carried them for me

When I was lost
in the deepest maze,
your tracks
led me back out

Later, with the jewels
of your serifs,
I fashioned crowns
for my beloveds

I struck your sulfured edges
against my heart;
your letters swept
like black birds across the sky,
ragged wings tipped
with gems
made of fire

Now, lifetimes older,
I've learned to read the fables
scratched out at your altars to truth

I've seen my relatives' names
entombed in the black books
of genocide

I know you as the weapon
whose steel dismembered
the bodies of my Ancestors,
inked fraudulent treaties
in a code we could not read

I have not forgotten
that you drew maps
like knives
across our Mother's body

I watch you now,
scavenging your own laws
for the right to rape
what's left:
water,
land,
women
the sacred

I watch as you scroll
yourself across a teleprompter
in glowing, luminous lies

I know better
than to trust you

Still, you swarm
through my blood,
Alphabet,
breed like a virus
in my bones,
crystalize
in my tears

Are you the handfuls of seeds
that feed me in famine,
or the embers of terror
burning my homeland?

Why can't I quit you?

Why do your clean faces
seduce me, your shiny black keys
coax my fingers into another dance
on your spikes?

Alphabet
I throw you out
onto the street,
scatter you on the wind

I hang you
on branches of oak,
break you
on the granite spine
of a mountain

Alphabet,
I gather you up
by the armful,

hold your splinters
against my breasts
like lost children

Your razor edges
lance despair,
drain the poison
you put there

Now you come to me
with an offer—
recompense
for all this history

You hold out
your elegant,
obsidian scars.
Oh, Alphabet—

give me that blade.

Weather Report

—for Philando Castile

It's 6:49 p.m., a warm southeastern day.
The neighbors next door host a corn-hole
competition in the alley, complete with beer,
charcoal grills and blue smoke, chairs
for the audience. *Another one bites*
the dust on the radio, deep bass throb.
Cigarette in her mouth, Granny braids
a little girl's hair, laughing low, husky.
Gramps walks slow up and down the alley,
baby in his arms. *Can't hurry love, you'll*
just have to wait, love don't come easy.

Green leaves hang heavy on the old black
walnut tree; uncut grass in spikey clumps,
quince bushes overflow with translucent
petals. The announcer sings: *No verdict*
for Philando. Can any of us breathe?
I never heard silence hang in the air
that loud. Then—*Thwack!* Bean bags hit
the board, hard. This game's been going on
as long as this family's lived on this street—
pre-Civil War, for sure. It's Father's Day
weekend. Confederate towns don't do
protests, no downtown gatherings,
no tears, no T.V. cameras.

Haul out the potato salad. Smash burgers
on the grill. Toss uncle another Diet Coke.
Flip a red bag up high in the air, catch it
behind your back. *Same old song.* Wring
out what joy this town still allows.

"No verdict"? In Virginia, that's like
a June weather report: 90 degrees.
89% humidity. Thunder. Lightning.
No verdict. Rain. *It's raining men.*

Fever

—for the house, and the spirits, at 203 S. Randolph St.

1.

I'm thinking of you tonight, Diego
and Jane Evans. Twilight eases over
my shoulders like an indigo cloak;
I walk past the two-over-two brick house
you built in the late 1840s—complete

with basement kitchen. Did the two of you
sit on that porch of a June evening, watch fireflies
play slow hide and seek over the graves
of the adjacent cemetery? It isn't famous
yet—Stonewall Jackson's headstone

is still granite inside a mountain, uncut;
Jackson himself tours New York,
visits Niagara Falls, reports for court
martial duty at Fort Ontario. You, Diego—
Black and free, successful merchant,

study law: Lexington isn't big enough
for you, your children, your dreams.
Do you see it coming, Jane—Civil War?
Your children's freedom fickle as lightning.
Colonization is the answer: to segregation,

discrimination, life confined on the Black
side of a small Southern town. You sell
your beautiful house on South Randolph
Street. Emigrate. You need a whole country,
one with a name you can ring like a bell.

You will settle for nothing less.

2.

List of Emigrants by the Liberia Packet, Capt. Howe, from
Norfolk, Va., January 26, 1850, for Monrovia and Bassa, Liberia:

No. 107 Diego Evans. 39. Trader. Reads. Free.
No.108 Jane, his wife. 30. Reads. Free.
No. 109 James H. F. 8. Reads. Free.
No. 110 Richard P. 7. Reads. Free.
No. 111 Lavinia Ann. 5. Free.
No. 112 John. 4. Free.

3.

Some interesting services were held at Lexington, Va.,
on the occasion of the departure of the emigrants

from that county. Our correspondent says,
"We had a farewell meeting on their account

on Wednesday the 19th in the Presbyterian
Church, which called a large audience. Col. Smith

of the Military Institute, and Rev. Dr. Junkin, President
of Washington College, addressed the congregation

in effective speeches on colonization; Maj. Preston
addressed the emigrants in very appropriate terms.

They were seated together on the right of the pulpit.
The Rev. W.S. White also addressed the meeting,

and led in prayer. Original hymns composed
for the occasion were sung; first by the people

led by the choir, and last by the emigrants.
The whole services were impressive,

and, I believe, of good effect for the cause."
signed, Miss Margaret Junkin.

4.

Not poor and empty-handed,
        as first to us they came,
With superstition branded,
        And want and woe and shame,—
Are we the race returning
        Back to their native sod,
But with our laws—our learning—
        Our freedom—and our God!

5.

Mary J. Henry, daughter of John V. Henry, writes
to friends in Lexington, "We rented a house on Broad

Street and Diego rented a house on the water side,
which all the old settlers told him not, but

he thought he could live there—being a good place
to sell his goods. But all his family took the fever.

We took the children home and they all got better,
but Diego and his wife departed this life."

6.

Ours may be a lot of trials,
        Bravely we will meet them all,
For the sake of our dear children,
        We will bear what may befall.

Dear Virginia! Dear Virginia!
        Loved, Oh loved, whe'er we roam,
Dear Virginia, loved Virginia!
        Farewell—farewell, dear old home.

7.

Liberia is like a fever, Diego;
colonization a contagion, Jane—

spread by fear of free Black
bodies walking unchained
through a white world,

a virus stoked by the Fugitive
Slave Act's long arm, a shadow
behind those bought or born free.
Frederick Douglass rails against
this "return" to Mother Africa,

fearing mass deportations—
Jane, do you watch your sons
and daughter sleep at night
in this house, await that loud
knock at the door? I wonder,

Diego, what is the difference
between Liberia and a reservation?
"Let us buy you a country,"
the American Colonization Society says,
"—sorry, sorry, for all that slavery mess—"

what they really mean: *slavery
for you is safety for us;
your freedom, our worst
nightmare.* They set this fever
on you, squeeze so hard

you have no place else to go.
Colonization is contagious.
Liberia is like
a fever. Catch it,
or be caught.

Transit of Venus

May 1769: a joint French/Spanish scientific commission sailed into Cabo San Lucas, Baja California, headed by Abbé Jean-Baptiste Chappe d'Auteroche, a Jesuit priest. Their purpose was to observe the transit of Venus on June 3rd.

Yellow fever. Matlazahuatl disease.
Black vomit. Typhus.
Spaniards, French, Natives alike
stricken by pestilence:
intense heat, insects,
an unnamed illness
gnaw away at the village
and the members
of our party,
but it is June 3, 1769,
and the passage
of Venus across the Sun's
bright disk will not happen again
for another 105 years.

I am consumed
by a superior fever
of cosmic origin.
For five hours,
the universe opens itself
to human inspection
of its divine architecture—
no physical malignance
can stand against Creation.

My companions and I unpack
delicate equipment
brought at dear expense
from Spain and France:
3-foot and 18-inch quadrants,
Berthold pendulum clock,

Dollond achromatic refrectors
all survive a battering transfer
from ship to blinding white sands.

We tear the roof off
an old corn storage building
built by Indians of the mission.
It will make a fine observatory.
The civilized world has much
to gain: we will be able
to calculate the precise parallax
of the sun, know where we are
in relation to the planets,
and God.
Delirious with fever,
headache like a spear
through the eye, I stare
through my telescope,
measure night after night:
instruments, stars
and satellite eclipses form
new constellations that guide
every move of aching limbs.
I place my records
in a small wooden box,
pray one of us will be spared
to carry these observations
back to Europe.

The village, the mission,
now ghost towns ransacked
and emptied by death.
Insects incessantly bite
and sting, try to eat us

before we relinquish
our mortal flesh.
Don Salvador de Medina
is almost dead; Don Vicente Doz
is very sick but through supreme
dedication to duty
finished his observations.
Alexandre-Jean Noël,
brave boy, promises he will paint
a record of my funeral, though
the priest is long since succumbed
and only a few naked Indians remain
to lay me in the earth.

I leave behind my legacy:
fair documentation
of a little dot crossing
the disk of the sun.

Indigenous Physics:
The Element Colonizatium

1.   The elimination of a substance from a living organism
     follows complex chemical kinetics.
     For example, the biological half-life
     of water in a human being
     is 9 to 10 days, with adjustments
     for behavior and temperature.
     A quantity of carbon-14 will decay
     to half its original amount after 5,730 years.
     After another 5,730 years,
     one-quarter of the original will remain.
     And so on.

     Obviously, the half-life of a substance
     depends upon the substance itself—
     measure for toxicity, fierceness, sheer venom.
     The research at hand for us today, then, is clear:
     what is the half-life of Colonizatium?
     Does Colonizatium reduce to half
     its initial impact in 500 years?
     In 1000 years?
     At what point
     does Colonizatium become unstable?
     Is the half-life of Colonizatium constant over the lifetime
     of an exponentially decaying
     Indigenous body?

2.   To quote a famous Indigenous physicist, *sometimes there are
     complications.*

     The decay of a mixture of two or more materials,
     which each decay exponentially but with different half-lives,
     is not exponential.
     Take nuclear waste.

Imagine a mixture of a rapidly decaying element A,
with a speedy half-life of 1 second, and more gradual
    decaying element B,
with a half-life of 1 year.
In minutes, almost all atoms of element A will have decayed
after repeated reductions by half, but
very few of the atoms of element B will have done so,
as only a small percentage of its half-life has elapsed. Thus,
the time taken for such a mixture to fall to half its original value
cannot be easily calculated.

The element Colonizatium is much like nuclear waste:
an unequal mixture of toxic events
with wildly different half-lives.
Start with invasion, war, starvation, rape, murder—
Indian boarding schools, reservations, outlawed religion,
shame.
Include an on-going bombardment of toxic events
over a period of decades:
termination, adopting-out, domestic violence, poverty,
substance addiction, incarceration rates, diabetes,
blood quantum debates, history books, mascots,
white shamanism, fake ndns,
anger.
A periodic table of traumatic elements.

3.   Given the difficulties
    in determining the half-life of Colonizatium,
    we might argue the necessity of redirecting
    our efforts into other
    more profitable calculations.
    However,
    despite the probalistic nature of the inquiry,

this as-yet-undiscovered formula
is thought to be paramount for our research
into a chronological prediction
of the Postcolonial state. Recent studies
indicate that the mixing of elements in unequal toxicities
and immeasurable psycho-social dynamics may best be gauged
not in mathematics
or statistics
or theoretical constructs,

but in the three Indigenous elements
Story, Dance, and Song.

In other words,
Deep Science of a precolonial origin
such as
formulas and algorithms encoded
within ceremonial circles, drums, or clapper sticks,
the spiraled helix notes of song,
diagrams of precise footsteps
on discrete portions of empowered earth;
stories plotted like fractal geometry,
the patterned asterisms of stars,
chemical kinetics hammered out
on the bodies of rocks.

Key to such explorations—
the reemergence
of a fourth Indigenous element:
Dreaming.
This component, long rumored to be permanently lost
or an unstable fantasy of treasure-hunters,
possesses shape-shifting abilities
that have allowed it to survive long periods of hibernation,
enabling structural recuperation and regeneration.

Preliminary work that combines Dreaming
with the three known elements
reveals two astonishing facts:

> First) a Postcolonizatium status is, in fact,
> impossible to achieve.

> Second) Story, Dance, Song and Dreaming
> neither calculate nor predict
> the half-life of Colonizatium.

Rather,
when applied to the Colonized subject,
these four elements
hasten decay of Colonizatium,
pull the heavy history into themselves,
break it down

the same way maize, mustard greens, pennycress,
sunflowers, blue sheep fescue, and canola
transform heavy metals.

The same way water hyacinths suck up mercury, lead, cadmium,
zinc, cesium, strontium-90, uranium,
and pesticides,

the same way bladder campion accumulates copper,
Indian mustard greens concentrate selenium, sulphur, chromium.

The same way willow, *Salix viminalis*, absorbs uranium and
petrochemicals.

And—
once the willow's biomass concentrates heavy metals,
once Story, Dance, Song and Dreaming do their work,
the willow rods must be woven
into baskets

in what might be called
a miraculous exponential,
were we not, of course, privy to the facts.

We must revise our aim, therefore, toward rapid
decay of Colonizatium,
or, De-Colonization.

4.   Start with Story.
Work your way
home.

Huwa.

When My Body Is the Archive

When my body is the archive,
strangers track ink all over
my grandmothers' language,
blot out the footprints of a million
souls from the edge of the continent;

stolen land stays stolen
even when thieves pluck
our Ancestors' names
from mission records,
sell *Tutuan* and *Malaxet*
online to those who want
all of the blessings,
none of the genocide.

At night, the archive falls into bed,
forgets to take her Metformin, dreams
about skeletons fleshed out
with salty genealogies,
a grandfather's bones rattling
inside mission walls
tapping out the succulent
syllables of old prayer
or a retroactive curse.

When my body is the archive
I sit down next to you
on that Lufthansa flight
to an Indigenous symposium
in Frankfurt, raise my hand
to ask about historical trauma,
interrupt your presentation on pre-contact
gender roles, throw your neon-red
dyed turkey feather headdress
on the floor and make you know:

this archive
was never inanimate,
this archive was never dead;
this archive was never
yours.

The Last Poem

—with thanks to Jorie Graham

Will the Last Poem know it's the last poem?
Will the Last Poem be written on paper,
or a wisp of smoke from ruins? How will we mark
her last breath? (And if the Last Poem comes
during our lifetime, will we be saved, or devoured?)

Will the Last Poem's alphabet be Japanese, Cherokee, English?
Cyrillic, Persian, petroglyph? Should the Last Poem's words
be spoken, or sung? Will anyone be left to hear?
Must the Last Poem be engraved in stone, scattered
on water, eaten for sustenance? Surely the Last Poem

will be a love poem. Won't it? That poem,
the Last Poem—will it be created by a human being,
or composed by poisoned rain and ash?
Are the lines falling into place even now? Has it found
the meter, placed the metaphor, set the type,

chosen the font, inked the press,
laid the paper? Has it favored rhyme
or slant, free or form, chant or psalm?
When the Last Poem reveals itself,
will our own words flare and flash into shapes
for the shapelessness to take back?

Prayer of Prayers

—for the Water Protectors at Standing Rock

The leaves hang on
into mid-November
oak, alder, locust—
each one a prayer flag
singing aloud—
scarlet, cinnamon, yellow
rippling with
wind's rough caress.

Every acorn,
every hickory nut,
a tobacco tie
hung in the trees;
they call out to us
come harvest your prayers.

Soon a blanket of prayers
will cover the earth
and the trees will stand
like prayer poles
dressed in feathers—
gifts from bluejay,
eagle, hummingbird,
meadowlark.
The planet prays for us,
for itself;
the planet sings
for November's endurance,
weaves a nest
for our future
to curl up inside
and learn winter's
Kevlar-wrapped stories.

This planet *is* a prayer.
Each icy night
under floodlights
and water cannons
she offers up moon
and stars, a holiness of cold.

You think prayer
cannot change this war?
Then redefine prayer:
it is clothing frozen
to the bodies of warriors
who do not carry
any weapon but sovereignty;
it is eyes swollen shut
with teargas, a relative
holding a bottle of saline solution;
it is the ferocious flower
left behind by a rubber bullet
blossoming on the face
of a woman
who is, in the end,
made wholly of prayer,
her spirit an impenetrable vessel
carrying devotion out to the edges
of camp where armed officers
try to hold prayer at bay,
as if prayer were a rabid bear
or a pack of wolves
that must be isolated,
beaten, eradicated
because prayer is contagious
prayer is *that* dangerous

prayer rages like a bonfire
no fire hose can quench.

The leaves hang on
into mid-November
oak, alder, locust—
each one a prayer flag
howling hoarse—
scarlet, cinnamon, yellow
snapping under
wind's cracked hands.
Every acorn,
every hickory nut,
a tobacco tie
swaying in the trees;
they cry out to us
come harvest your prayers
come pound them into meal
come mix them with river water
come cook them on this blazing rock:

People, come feast
on this prayer so righteous
it burns your tongues,
wash it down
with a sip from the river
whose songs will always call you
Beloved.

Special thanks to . . .

- My son Danny, who helped me determine the appropriate Latin nomenclature for a time-traveling turtle in "Eastern Box Turtle." We knew that Classics degree was a good idea!
- My daughter Miranda, who told me "You'd better write that down, Mom!" after hearing the shuttle driver's story in "What the Shuttle Driver Told Me."
- Laya Kovitch, whose small altar of broken things inspired a poem, then a book.
- Karenne Wood, for the Monacan word for river in "Taksita."

Those whose words and spirits support and lift my own. There are many, but especially, C. Rosalind Bell, Kimberly Blaeser, Natalie Diaz, Heid Erdrich, CMarie Fuhrman, Joy Harjo, Ernestine Saankalaxt' Hayes, Linda Hogan, Suzanne Parker Keen, Ursula K. Le Guin, Janet McAdams, Craig Santos Perez, Georgiana Sanchez, Cheryl Savageau, Linda Rodriguez, Ire'ne Lara Silva, TC Tolbert, T.J. Tallie, Dan Vera and Peter Montgomery.

- The staff at Pronto Gelateria Café, especially Tequlia Cooper, who anticipate my order, share gossip and solidarity, and create, every day, the writing home I didn't know I needed. Many of these poems were drafted and/or workshopped with Julie Phillips Brown at "our" table, with one of your beautiful lattes in hand.
- Daman Reynolds, for guidance and re-membering.
- Chance, best and loyal dog, who accompanied me many a morning on porches by rivers, streets, and ponds as I wrote, or sprawled on the rug beside my chair for hours of teaching and writing, and who taught me by example the pleasures of a sweet breeze, the perfect angle of sunshine, and the sheer bliss of being alive. I miss you every day, Mr. Dancer.
- Julie Philips Brown, dear Writing Buddy, whose friendship and poetry continue to be a lifeline and a blessing.
- Margo Solod: wife, friend and dearest anchor. All my gratitude for sharing your gifts and life with me.

And thanks to Ben Furnish, editor extraordinaire, whose dedication to poetry and poets cannot be measured. This book exists because you, kindest and gentlest of men, fought fiercely for these poems. Nimasianexelpasaleki.

Publication Acknowledgments

The following poems have been published (sometimes in earlier versions) in the following places:

"Acorn" and "Kakalu-ichi" *News from Native California, Best American Poetry Blog*

"My Crow" *A Bird Black as the Sun: California Poets on Crows & Ravens*

"What Whales Want" *Tending the Fire: Native Voices and Portraits*

"Prayer of Prayers" *Orion*

"Eastern Box Turtle" *A Literary Field Guide to Southern Appalachia* (University of Georgia Press 2019)

"When You Forget Me," "Love in the Margins," and "Palimpsest" in *LitHub*

"Tears of the Sun," Native Voices: Indigenous American Poetry, Craft and Conversations (Tupelo Press)

"When My Body Is the Archive" and "Indigenous Physics: The Element Colonizatium" in *American Culture and Research Journal.*

"Indigenous Physics: The Element Colonizatium" for Joy Harjo's online Poet Laureate project,"Living Nations, Living Words: A Map of First Peoples Poetry."

Notes:

"How to Love the Burning World":

The epigraph is from Barry Lopez's beautiful essay, "Love in a Time of Terror: On Natural Landscapes, Metaphorical Living, and Warlpiri Identity," published on LitHub.

"That Word":

Mary TallMountain's poem, "There Is No Word for Goodbye," from her collection *The Light on the Tent Wall*, spoke to me as a source of comfort during a difficult parting, and brought me back to dwell on that word.

"Hagiography":

A line from Kimiko Hahn's poem "Admission"—"Cathedral of childhood"— broke me open, and this poem fell out.

"When You Forget Me":

Pablo Neruda's poem, "If You Forget Me" struck a nerve.

"Bee Balm":

Linda Hogan's essay "Walking," in *The Woman Who Watches Over the World*, contains the line "You are the result of the love of thousands." I wanted to give those words back to her in this poem.

"After Charlottesville":

Writer C. Rosalind Bell's comment that "We are the grownups now," in response to the incident in Charlottesville, Virginia in which Heather Heyer was killed by a car driven into the peaceful protest she was attending, haunted me.

"The Last Poem":

A line from Jorie Graham's poem "What the End is For" resonated with me late one night: "shapes the shapelessness was taking back." Her poem, layered with the bruises of endings, fuels my own musings on last things.

An enrolled member of the Ohlone-Costanoan Esselen Nation of California, poet Deborah A. Miranda was born in Los Angeles to an Esselen/Chumash father and a mother of European ancestry. She grew up in Washington State, earned a BS in teaching moderate special-needs children from Wheelock College in 1983 and an MA and PhD in English from the University of Washington in 2001.

Miranda's collections of poetry include *Raised by Humans* (2015); *Indian Cartography: Poems* (1999), winner of the Diane Decorah Memorial First Book Award from the Native Writers' Circle of the Americas; and *The Zen of La Llorona* (2005), nominated for a Lambda Literary Award. Miranda also received the 2000 Writer of the Year Award for Poetry from the Wordcraft Circle of Native Writers and Storytellers. Her mixed-genre collection *Bad Indians: A Tribal Memoir* (2013) won a Gold Medal from the Independent Publisher's Association and the PEN Oakland Josephine Miles Literary Award, and was shortlisted for the William Saroyan Award.

She is Thomas H. Broadus, Jr. professor of English at Washington and Lee University.

BkMk Press is grateful for the support it has recently received
from the following organizations and individuals:

Missouri Arts Council
Miller-Mellor Foundation
Neptune Foundation
Richard J. Stern Foundation for the Arts
Stanley H. Durwood Foundation
William T. Kemper Foundation

Beverly Burch
Jaimee Wriston Colbert
Maija Rhee Devine
Whitney and Mariella Kerr
Carla Klausner
Lorraine M. López
Patricia Cleary Miller
Margot Patterson
Alan Proctor
James Hugo Rifenbark
Roderick and Wyatt Townley